S0-BEJ-335

ideals®
THANKSGIVING
2005

*Dedicated to a celebration of the American ideals
of faith in God, loyalty to country, and love of family.*

Features

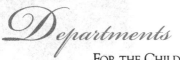
Departments

*Cover: A pumpkin, bright flowers, and a vibrant red and gold
carpet of leaves beneath an adirondack chair form an autumn still
life on a sunny afternoon. Photograph by William H. Johnson.*

*Inside front cover: Swans glide through the soft glow
of the reflecting pool on a tranquil autumn afternoon
in this painting by Eugéne Chigot (1860–1927) entitled
A WALK BY THE RIVER ON AN AUTUMN DAY. Image from
Fine Art Photographic Library, Ltd., London/Private Collection.*

IDEALS—Vol. 62, No. 5, September 2005 IDEALS (ISSN
0019-137X, USPS 256-240) is published six times a year:
January, March, May, July, September, and November by
Ideals Publications, a division of Guideposts, 39 Seminary
Hill Road, Carmel, NY 10512. Copyright © 2005 by Ideals
Publications, a division of Guideposts. All rights reserved.
The cover and entire contents of IDEALS are fully protected
by copyright and must not be reproduced in any manner
whatsoever. Title IDEALS registered U.S. Patent Office.
Printed and bound in USA. Printed on Weyerhaeuser
Husky. The paper used in this publication meets the mini-
mum requirements of American National Standard for
Information Sciences—Permanence of Paper for Printed
Library Materials, ANSI Z39.48-1984. Periodicals postage
paid at Carmel, New York, and additional mailing offices.
Canadian mailed under Publications Mail Agreement
Number 40010140. POSTMASTER: Send address changes
to IDEALS, 39 Seminary Hill Road, Carmel, NY 10512.
CANADA POST: Send address changes to Guideposts
PO Box 1051, Fort Erie ON L2A 6C7. For subscription or
customer service questions, contact Ideals Publications, a
division of Guideposts, 39 Seminary Hill Road, Carmel,
NY 10512. Fax 845-228-2115. Reader Preference Service:
We occasionally make our mailing lists available to other
companies whose products or services might interest you.
If you prefer not to be included, please write to IDEALS
Customer Service.

ISBN 0-8249-1304-3 GST 893989236

Visit the *Ideals* website
at www.idealsbooks.com

SIGNS OF FALL

Maxine McCray Miller

The months pass swiftly, and I see
Bright yellow heads of goldenrod
Where tinted apple blossoms blew
Against the sweetly smelling sod.

Frost powders pumpkins on the vines
And crowns the hills with diamond hoar;
Each blossomed bush contrives to show
More brilliant dress than blooms it wore.

Bright autumn leaves drift slowly down,
A carpet for the courts of fall;
The cold winds whisper and rehearse
The coming season's ritual.

As summer steps beyond the last
Dividing mountain tipped with blue,
I gather memories of her hours
For fireplace flames to light anew.

A golden afternoon is an invitation to pause amid preparations for the winter in this painting by Charles Clair (1860–1930) entitled LE MOISSON. Image from Fine Art Photographic Library, Ltd., London/Waterhouse & Dodd.

SILENCE

Edna Jaques

I like the silence of old fields at night,
    The peace of evening, dawn's attendant hush,
Mother-of-pearl inlaid against the sky,
    As if a master hand with careful brush
Stippled the sky as women often do,
    Tinting their kitchen walls in rose and blue.

I like a quiet place where no rude voice
    Shatters the silence into quivering sound,
Where hostas grow in graceful heaps
    And outline green carpets on the ground,
Where wild olive trees leaning by a pool
    Wave silver wands to children by the school.

I love the peace of Sunday afternoons,
    The calm well-being of a day of rest,
Where men walk idly out around the barns,
    Clean shaven, garbed in all their Sunday best.
Even the cattle seem to sense the day
    And walk sedately on their homeward way.

I like the silence of an autumn woods
    Before the russet leaves begin to fall,
The utter stillness of a prairie night,
    As if it slept in some eternal thrall,
A willing prisoner held in Beauty's sway,
    Dreaming the quiet centuries away.

Autumn in the Country

Earle J. Grant

Milkweeds spin silver in the sun,
Goldenrods toss their gilded heads,
Grapes are staining vines with purple,
Chrysanthemums glow in garden beds.

Pears are hanging golden lanterns,
The apple trees flaunt crimson tints,
Corn shocks are stitched on tawny fields,
Bold marigolds spill haunting scents.

In new bouffant skirts of yellow,
Maples dance down the autumn scene;
Mist is draping the topaz hills
In a scarf with an argent sheen.

Suddenly the country silence
Is broken by an enchanting cry.
I turn my eyes to the heavens;
Wild geese, in a V, are passing by!

Oh, I am left almost breathless
As I behold the distant sight
And wish to join the feathered hosts
In their trackless southward flight.

Then I discover a red sumac,
A burning bush standing near;
And wanderlust departs from me:
There is too much loveliness here.

A Song of Autumn

Edith Fassler

I walked out in the field today
And heard the song of autumn play;
I found the golden kernels there
Beneath the husk of ripening air.

I could not estimate the yield,
The moneyed value of the field,
But found sustaining beauty there
And in the heart a thankful prayer.

*Pumpkins filled with zinnias, goldenrod, dahlias, and sunflowers provide
a decorative centerpiece for seasonal celebrations. Photograph by Gay Bumgarner.*

5

Wild Wings
Ruby Stover

Wild wings! Beautiful wings! Whirring by
In the silver silence of a leaden sky,
Wending your way to a southland home,
Lifting my heart to heights unknown.
O ceaseless Watcher on Thy throne on high,
Must my heart ever ache when wild geese fly?
Grant me the courage Thy love can impart
To earth-bound feet but a skyward heart.

Song of Faith
Stella Craft Tremble

O singing wren, alone in this cold field
At autumn turn of equinox,
Summer has gone: do you not hear
The blackbirds gossiping in flocks?

You think a song may keep away the cold?
Do you not hear the wild geese cry
Or see the northern leaden clouds?
Winter will fall from darkened sky.

Your April song will not keep snow away
Or make the bladed winds depart;
Yet, thank you for your song of faith:
Spring lingers in a singing heart.

*In North Cascades National Park in Washington,
huckleberry bushes accent the alpine meadows
of Cascade Pass. Photograph by Mary Liz
Austin/Donnelly Austin Photography.*

October

Robert Frost

O hushed October morning mild,
Thy leaves have ripened to the fall;
Tomorrow's wind, if it be wild,
Should waste them all.
The crows above the forest call;
Tomorrow they may form and go.
O hushed October morning mild,
Begin the hours of this day slow.
Make the day seem to us less brief.
Hearts not averse to being beguiled,
Beguile us in the way you know.
Release one leaf at break of day;
At noon release another leaf;
One from our trees, one far away.
Retard the sun with gentle mist;
Enchant the land with amethyst.
Slow, slow!
For the grapes' sake, if they were all,
Whose leaves already are burnt with frost,
Whose clustered fruit must else be lost—
For the grapes' sake along the wall.

*A white picket fence and autumn leaves surround the Robert Frost
Farm in Derry, New Hampshire. Photograph by William H. Johnson.*

Goldsmiths

Sudie Stuart Hager

The wondrous shine on autumn leaves
Must be the golden notes
That beat on them the summer through
From songbirds' rapturous throats.

Autumn's Arrival

Dean Robbins

Now look, and see that autumn has arrived
On chariots of wind racing the sun.
Regrettably, summer has not survived;
But what remains is beautifully done.

Awake to mornings trimmed in icy lace,
To azure skies holding parades of white.
The risen sun now keeps a lower place
In its attempt to warm with weaker light.

Midday's for walking through the wooded hills
Aflame with bursts of yellow, orange, red;
And up ahead a flood of asters spills
As blue as any sky draped overhead.

Sundown announces cool, clear, starry nights.
Wood-smoke aroma fills the evening air
As flocks of geese begin their southern flights
Through moonlit skies and bid, "Goodbye. Take care."

Now look, for autumn waits outside your door.
The final fling before a winter's sleep
Brings with it all that makes us wish for more,
Then flees as naught but memories to keep.

Quicksilver

Mildred Keiser

You can't hold magic in your hands
Or touch a memory
Or lock a sunset in a room
Where it will always be.
But when you see October start,
If you are one like me,
You want the shining afternoons
To last for all eternity.
You want the sumac's splash of fire
And soft winds to ever blow;
And though the splendor
        breaks your heart,
You cannot let it go.
You want each glorious day preserved;
You long to hold them fast;
Your soul oftentimes yearns to keep
Those things that cannot last.

*Pinot noir grapes cling to a bronze-leaved
vine in the Red Hills of Yamhill County,
Oregon. Photograph by Steve Terrill.*

FOR THE CHILDREN

Leaving

Eileen Spinelli

"We are leaving," say the leaves.
I hear, "Goodbye!"
They twirl from branches,
    skip through sky,
    gather lightly
    at my feet,
    skitter brightly
    down the street:
    golden yellow,
    red, and brown,
    swirling up and
    out of town.
The breezes sing an autumn song,
    and like the leaves,
    I dance along.

But I won't say goodbye!
    Oh, no.
Come winter, I will dance
    in snow!

Art by Russ Flint.

Autumn

Emily Dickinson

The morns are meeker than they were,
    The nuts are getting brown;
The berry's cheek is plumper,
    The rose is out of town.

The maple wears a gayer scarf,
    The field a scarlet gown.
Lest I should be old-fashioned,
    I'll put a trinket on.

Hickory Nut Hunting

Ruth H. Underhill

Down on Grandpa's farm,
Just when it was fall,
Back to the timber we would go
Where hickory trees were tall.

We'd take along our burlap bags
For hickory nuts to fill;
We'd search the ground so carefully,
Up and down the hills.

Now and then we'd find a leaf
Of lovely shaded hue;
We'd pick it up and keep it close
And carry more home too.

After our bags were more than filled
And the nuts were safe from harm,
We'd trudge over the final hill
Across our Grandpa's farm.

The colors of autumn flow across the slopes and valleys near Newfound Gap in the Smoky Mountains. Photograph by Mary Liz Austin/Donnelly Austin Photography.

Bittersweet Time

Earle J. Grant

When October days grow crisp
    And painted leaves clothe hills,
We take our baskets and follow
    The mountain trails and flowing rills
To where bittersweet profusely
    Grows along an old stone fence;
It sates our hunger for beauty
    With its vivid orange tints.
The sky above is gentian blue;
    Winds sweep, sharp as peppermint;
Fox grapes hang in purple clusters;
    We feast on their spicy scent.
We cut ripe sprays of bittersweet,
    Lovely beyond all measure.
Then we head down the mountainside,
    Grateful and filled with pleasure.

Shaker boxes and chinaberry branches fill a deep window seat in this country home. Photograph by Jessie Walker.

Inset: The vibrant red and gold of bittersweet berries mimic the colors of autumn leaves. Photograph by LeFever/Grushow/Grant Heilman.

Overleaf: Birch and maple trees color the lakeshore in red and gold in Ottawa National Forest, Michigan. Photograph by Carr Clifton.

A Summons

Georgia B. Adams

I'm called by the flaming forest
To walk these October days
Down old, familiar footpaths,
Among its leafy maze.

Verdant trees in all their glory
Change robes almost overnight;
And their transfiguration brings
New colors, pure and bright.

I see a squirrel, quick and lively,
Scamper through the fallen leaves.
As always in this season,
My heart gladly receives

So much of the cup of beauty
From the Master Artist's hand,
Scenes of the flaming forest
Scattered throughout the land.

I'm called by the flaming forest;
I'm called and my feet must stray
Down old, familiar footpaths
On this gold October day.

Indian Summer

Mildred L. Jarrell

The last of Indian summer still remains
And spreads its golden warmth upon the hills.
The valley slopes show spires of crimson flame;
Throughout the land a russet carpet spills.

The last of Indian summer fills the air.
A hazy wreath enfolds the highest pine;
The scent of woody smoke is everywhere,
And memories of bonfires come to mind.

The last of Indian summer's on the fields
Where shocks of corn stand watch with
          pumpkins bright.
Soon all gives way to chill and quickly yields
To early frost that whispers through the night.

*Cherry leaves rest on a bed of petunias in Multnomah
County, Oregon. Photograph by Steve Terrill.*

I Love the Wind

Grace V. Watkins

I love a little prankster wind
That scampers on a plain.
I love a grass-and-clover wind,
Sweet smelling after rain.
But more than either one, I love
A quiet wind that sings
Of sun and orioles and all
The lovely golden things.
For, oh, it always seems to me
A quiet wind and I
Are thanking God for meadowland
And autumn hills and sky.

*The blackbird whirled
in the autumn winds.
It was a small part
of the pantomime.*
—WALLACE STEVENS

Autumn Winds

Helen B. Trentadue

When autumn winds whisper softly,
They scatter dead leaves of care
By quiet meadows and byways.
They brush the tall aspen with gold
And hint of the secrets summer has told.
When autumn winds whisper softly,
They creep toward the orchard with red
And brush gossamer purple on hills.
Earth's brow is peaceful and still,
When autumn winds whisper softly.

The majesty of Grand Portal Point on Lake Superior is part of the beauty of Pictured Rocks National Lakeshore in Michigan. Photograph by Carr Clifton.

Apple Song

Frances Frost

The apples are seasoned
And ripe and sound.
Gently they fall
On the yellow ground.

The apples are stored
In the dusky bin
Where hardly a glimmer
Of light creeps in.

In the firelit, winter
Nights, they'll be
The clear sweet taste
Of a summer tree!

**I should like to rise and go
Where the golden apples grow.**
—Robert Louis Stevenson

Gathering Autumn

Lucile Coleman

In baskets near the apples' russet roar,
Thanksgiving pumpkins and cranberries share
The cider air well spiced with holiday;
And geese cut southward through an unmarked lane.
The trees weave Indian summer out of sleep;
White clouds roam and scatter like wild young sheep;
We gather autumn in a golden heap.

*A basket of apples and autumn leaves creates a festive dining
room table. Photograph by Chad Ehlers/Grant Heilman.*

eyes and the tang of valley orchards for your nose. . . . —Carl Sandburg

Pumpkins

Kay Hoffman

I like to see a garden patch
With pumpkins big and small.
I like to see them heaped up high
When comes the season fall.

Beside a friendly lamppost
Or in windows on my street,
I like to see them smiling
On a night of trick or treat.

No matter where I see them,
They bring a happy sigh.
But most of all, I like them
In a warm pumpkin pie.

Your Pumpkin

Jean Adams

The day you brought the pumpkin home
The air was spiced and clear,
Dry leaves rattled when they blew,
And the sky was blue and near.

The pumpkins seemed much bigger then
Than those one might see now.
And pumpkins picked out in the field
Beat store-bought ones somehow.

So when I crunch through leaves at fall
In frosted air at night,
I'm back where pumpkins were bigger,
And the sky was blue and bright.

Pumpkins dot the fields, geese float through the sky, and haystacks are neatly arranged, reflecting a serene autumn scene in this painting by Bob Pettes entitled PARKVILLE PUMPKINS.

27

Come Gently

Dorothea Spears Botha

Come slowly, Winter.
Give us time to prune the tree and cut the wood
And stack it tidily away,
As wise men do.
Let us gather in the harvests that shall be
    our food
And boughs of scarlet berries that shall keep
    our houses gay.

Come gently, Winter.
Leave the lovely leaves of gold
And red and brown on the bough
A little while.
Dissuade the rude hand of the tempest
    from tearing
Trusting trees too suddenly,
Leaving them shocked and shaken,
    stripped and bare,
Forsaken.
Rather, let the leaves drop one by one
Still fair, as now,
Into the Indian summer air.

All things have something
   more than barren use;
There is a scent upon the brier,
A tremulous splendor
   in the autumn dews;
Cold morns are fringed with fire.
           —Alexander Smith

*Snow lightly dusts the trees on the Appalachian Trail
in White Mountain National Forest, Laconia,
New Hampshire. Photograph by William H. Johnson.*

BACKYARD CALENDAR

Joan Donaldson

I pull my coat collar up as the north wind hums through the weathered board fence that encloses my garden. Tonight a hard frost is predicted. Sometime after midnight, the wind will cease and frost will form and blacken all plant life. An earlier light frost nipped the squash vines and hardened the skins of the fruit, so they will store well in our root cellar.

Methodically, I heap a mound of tan butternut, dark green buttercups, and striped sweet dumpling squash into my garden cart. It was only four months ago, under a searing sun, that I shoveled compost into this cart. That afternoon, I daydreamed of iced tea while I mulched each squash plant. But the back of my mind held the image of this harvest.

Gardeners tend to work with a vision of future abundance, and they store away the best memories from each season. Now I must labor with an eye on the falling mercury. Like the proverbial ant, I have spent hours digging potatoes or shelling dry beans; yet I know this evening is the moment of reckoning. Everything I wish to save must either be removed or covered before I retreat to sit by the fire.

I have already cleared patches of the garden of darkened tomato and withered pepper plants. The sand-colored leaves on the cornstalks rustle in the breeze; some stalks are bent from raiding raccoons that gleaned the nubbins. Having picked all the squash, I cut down the corn and align the stalks in a pile.

Although corn shocks traditionally provide fodder for cattle, I erect one each year purely for decoration. I stand it up next to the maroon-stained garden shed and position a few squash at its base. Like a festive banner, the corn shock will welcome visitors and celebrate these last days of harvesting.

And yet one bed in the garden defies the dwindling daylight and the north wind. Short rows of Savoy cabbage, broccoli, and mounds of red radicchio thrive in these cool autumn weeks. Carefully, I drape a blanket over the broccoli and cabbage to ward off tonight's chill. I also carry over the windows to my cold frames and plop them onto the silver boards that pro-

Like handfuls of garnets tossed into the bushes, the rosehips will soon be the only brilliant color in the garden.

tect a patchwork of red and green lettuce seedlings. As I pick up the last window, I survey the roses surrounding the garden.

Several rose canes still sport green leaves; and near the top of a seven-foot bush, a few pink blossoms have escaped the early frosts. Behind them the red and gold sassafras leaves glow in the slanted afternoon sunlight that also illuminates the cherry red rosehips. Like handfuls of garnets tossed into the bushes, the rosehips will soon be the only brilliant color in the

Fall perennials and assorted pumpkins are gathered together for festive display in this garden. Photograph by Jane Grushow/Grant Heilman.

garden. A few dusty purple asters linger; but tonight will bring their demise too, so I snip these few roses and asters for the last bouquet of the year.

Joan Donaldson is the author of a picture book and a young adult novel, as well as essays that have appeared in many national publications. She and her husband raised their sons on Pleasant Hill Farm in Michigan, where they continue to practice rural skills.

November Gold

Ann Schneider

Come, let us stroll hand in hand
And watch fall traipse across the land.
Trees are losing verdant leaves;
New colors come as summer flees.
Something marvelous takes place
When leaves spiral in whirling grace;
Their tawny yellows, reds, and browns
Deprive trees of their courtly gowns.
What joy to walk through golden leaves.
Behold a lone leaf as it cleaves,
Reluctant to make its descent;
It clings to hope until the end.
Autumn gathers leaves in her fold;
Suddenly streets are paved with gold.
Come forth this autumn day and know
The wealth of nature's greatest show.
The wondrous magic of the season
Enchants with every new fall sun.

Twilight

J. Harold Gwynne

The rim of the moon is shining high,
A lovely form in the vesper sky,
A perfect crescent of mellow light,
A jewel to clasp the robe of night.

The halcyon Indian summer day
In colorful twilight fades away;
The sky is aglow with rosy gold,
While shadows deep the hills enfold:

A hallowed time to be still and feel
The presence of God so very real,
A time to center one's thoughts above
And rest secure in His perfect love.

O Will Divine, at the heart of all,
Permit Thy healing mercies fall;
Reveal Thy grace in all things best,
And help us know Thy perfect rest.

Black oaks are touched by golden sunlight in Yosemite National Park, California. Photograph by Carr Clifton.

Definition

Edith Shaw Butler

A house is built of joists and beams,
Of sturdy sills so thick,
Of rafters pointing to the sky,
Clapboards, and mortared brick.

A home is built of comradeship
And moments shared by you:
Strength of a man, a woman's love,
Time spent with family too.

A home is built from bits of song,
Batter in earthen bowls,
A kettle and a glowing fire,
Sweet milk and buttered rolls,

A rocking chair, a row of books,
Bright flowers in brown loam;
A house must have a building lot;
One room can hold a home.

Forever on
Thanksgiving Day
The heart will find
the pathway home.
—Wilbur D. Nesbit

A tree-lined avenue is a lovely backdrop for an autumn stroll.
Photograph by Larry LeFever/Grant Heilman.

Coming Home

Patience Strong

Coming home at close of day,
Trouble fades and slips away.
Coming home the world looks kind,
With work and worry left behind.
On the homeward way again,
After all the fret and strain,
Roll on wheels along the track;
Happy thought, I'm coming back,
Back to that familiar street.
Hurry, hurry, weary feet;
Take me to that homely door;
That is what I'm yearning for.
There I'll find my heart's desire—
Quiet and dreams beside the fire,
Comfort and a cozy chair,
And somebody special waiting there.
So when life's last journey ends,
And my soul's last prayer ascends
Up to heaven's starry dome,
May I feel I'm coming home.

*Home is the place where character is built,
where sacrifices to contribute to the happiness
of others are made, and where love has
taken up its abode.* —Elijah Kellogg

A wide front porch welcomes visitors to the Crystal Bell Bed and Breakfast in Wabeno, Wisconsin. Photograph by Darryl E. Beers.

A MODEL OF CHRISTIAN CHARITY

John Winthrop

Written and delivered in 1630 by John Winthrop, who would become the first governor of Massachusetts, aboard the Arabella *as it voyaged to the New World.*

We are a company professing ourselves fellow members of Christ, in which respect only though we were absent from each other many miles and had our employments as far distant, yet we ought to account ourselves knit together by this bond of love, and live in the exercise of it, if we would have comfort of our being in Christ. . . .

It is by a mutual consent, through a special overvaluing providence and a more than an ordinary approbation of the Churches of Christ, to seek out a place of cohabitation and Consortship under a due form of Government both civil and ecclesiastical. In such cases as this, the care of the public must oversway all private respects, by which, not only conscience, but mere civil policy doth bind us. For it is a true rule that particular Estates cannot subsist in the ruin of the public.

The end is to improve our lives to do more

We must be willing to abridge ourselves of our superfluities for the supply of other's necessities.

---

service to the Lord; the comfort and increase of the body of Christ, whereof we are members; that ourselves and posterity may be the better preserved from the common corruptions of this evil world, to serve the Lord and work out our Salvation under the power and purity of His holy ordinances. . . .

Whatsoever we did or ought to have done when we lived in England, the same must we do, and more also, where we go. That which the most in their churches maintain as truth in profession only, we must bring into familiar and constant practice; as in this duty of love, we must love brotherly without dissimulation; we must love one another with a pure heart fervently. We must bear one another's burdens. . . .

The Lord hath given us leave to draw our own articles. We have professed to enterprise these and those accounts, upon these and those ends. We have hereupon besought Him of favor and blessing. Now if the Lord shall please to hear us and bring us in peace to the place we desire, then hath He ratified this covenant and sealed our Commission and will expect a strict performance of the articles contained in it; but if we shall neglect the observation of these articles which are the ends we have propounded, and, dissembling with our God, shall fall to embrace this present world and prosecute our carnal intentions, seeking great things for ourselves and our posterity, the Lord will surely break out in wrath against us; be revenged of such a [sinful] people and make us know the price of the breach of such a covenant.

Now the only way to avoid this shipwreck, and to provide for our posterity, is to follow the counsel of Micah, "to do justly, to love mercy, to walk humbly with our God." For this end, we must be knit together, in this work, as one man. We must entertain each other in brotherly affection. We must be willing to abridge ourselves of our superfluities for the supply of other's necessities. We must uphold a familiar commerce together in all meekness, gentleness, patience, and liberality.

The Landing of the Pilgrims. Lithograph by Currier and Ives. Image from Art Resource, NY/Giraudon.

We must delight in each other; make other's conditions our own; rejoice together, mourn together, labor and suffer together, always having before our eyes our commission and community in the work, as members of the same body. So shall we "keep the unity of the spirit in the bond of peace."

For we must consider that we shall be as a city upon a hill.

The Lord will be our God and delight to dwell among us, as His own people, and will command a blessing upon us in all our ways so that we shall see much more of His wisdom, power, goodness, and truth, than formerly we have been acquainted with. We shall find that the God of Israel is among us when ten of us shall be able to resist a thousand of our enemies; when He shall make us a praise and glory that men shall say of succeeding plantations, "The Lord make it likely that of New England." For we must consider that we shall be as a city upon a hill. The eyes of all people are upon us. So that if we shall deal falsely with our God in this work we have undertaken, and so cause Him to withdraw His present help from us, we shall be made a story and a by-word through the world. We shall open the mouth of enemies to speak evil of the ways of God, and all professors for God's sake. We shall shame the faces of many of God's worthy servants and cause their prayers to be turned into curses upon us till we be consumed out of the good land whither we are going.

Therefore let us choose life that we and our seed may live by obeying His voice and cleaving to Him, for He is our life and our prosperity.

THE OLD NEW ENGLAND THANKSGIVING

Harriet Beecher Stowe

When the apples were all gathered and the cider was all made, and the yellow pumpkins were rolled in from many a hill in billows of gold, and the corn was husked, and the labors of the season were done, and the warm, late days of Indian summer came in, dreamy, and calm, and still, with just enough frost to crisp the ground of a morning, but with warm traces of benignant, sunny hours at noon, there came over the community a sort of genial repose of spirit—a sense of something accomplished and of a new golden mark made in advance—and the deacon began to say to the minister, of a Sunday, "I suppose it's about time for the Thanksgiving proclamation."

Sugar maples frame this vista of East Topsham, Vermont.
Photograph by William H. Johnson.

Thanksgiving on the Farm

Starrlette L. Howard

The years go passing by;
Some flood my heart to make it warm,
But nothing seems to surpass
Memories of Thanksgiving on the farm.

Each one had his chores to do,
But they were done with zest;
All knew the house would soon welcome
And hold so many beloved guests.

The smells of squash and cornbread,
And the turkey as it browned,
And a fire in the fireplace
Would greet the guests from town.

Around the long, old table
The relatives gathered there;
But the feast could not begin
Until Grandfather offered prayer.

And children knew the afternoon
Would be open to play
In gold and brown, dry, brittle fields
Or upon the bales of hay.

Sometimes toward the evening
Gentle snowflakes fell,
And sweet pumpkin pies were served
With old stories to retell.

*Chrysanthemums and pumpkins fill an old wagon in
this autumn display in Jackson, New Hampshire.
Photograph by William H. Johnson.*

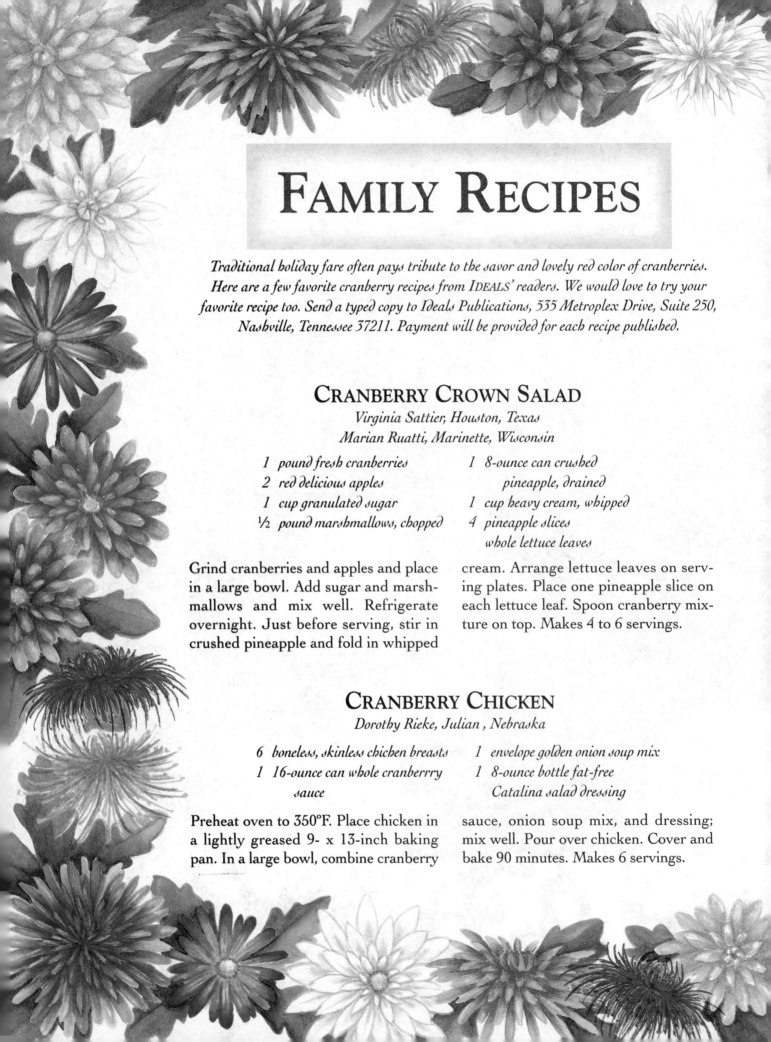

FAMILY RECIPES

Traditional holiday fare often pays tribute to the savor and lovely red color of cranberries. Here are a few favorite cranberry recipes from IDEALS' readers. We would love to try your favorite recipe too. Send a typed copy to Ideals Publications, 535 Metroplex Drive, Suite 250, Nashville, Tennessee 37211. Payment will be provided for each recipe published.

CRANBERRY CROWN SALAD

Virginia Sattier, Houston, Texas
Marian Ruatti, Marinette, Wisconsin

1 pound fresh cranberries
2 red delicious apples
1 cup granulated sugar
½ pound marshmallows, chopped
1 8-ounce can crushed
   pineapple, drained
1 cup heavy cream, whipped
4 pineapple slices
   whole lettuce leaves

Grind cranberries and apples and place in a large bowl. Add sugar and marshmallows and mix well. Refrigerate overnight. Just before serving, stir in crushed pineapple and fold in whipped cream. Arrange lettuce leaves on serving plates. Place one pineapple slice on each lettuce leaf. Spoon cranberry mixture on top. Makes 4 to 6 servings.

CRANBERRY CHICKEN

Dorothy Rieke, Julian , Nebraska

6 boneless, skinless chichen breasts
1 16-ounce can whole cranberrry
   sauce
1 envelope golden onion soup mix
1 8-ounce bottle fat-free
   Catalina salad dressing

Preheat oven to 350°F. Place chicken in a lightly greased 9- x 13-inch baking pan. In a large bowl, combine cranberry sauce, onion soup mix, and dressing; mix well. Pour over chicken. Cover and bake 90 minutes. Makes 6 servings.

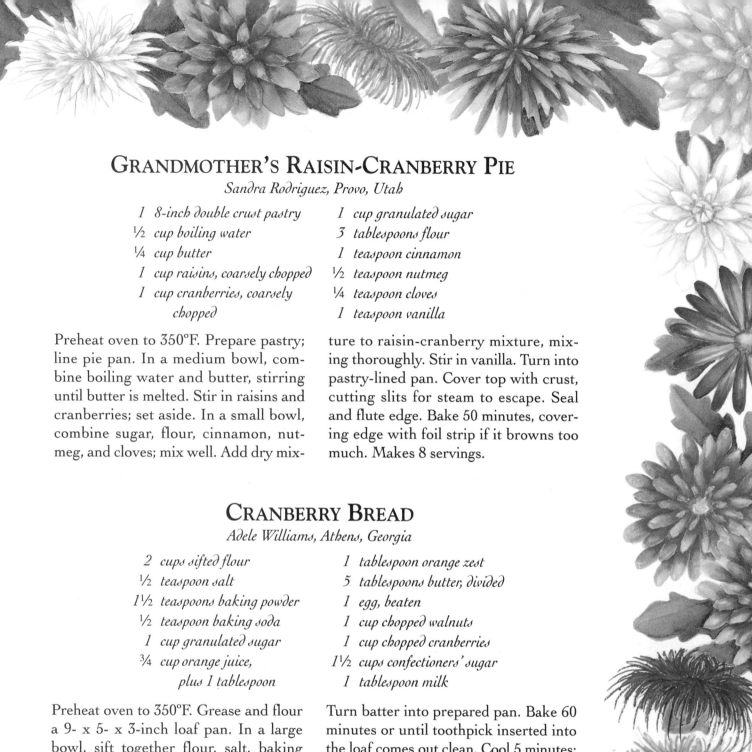

GRANDMOTHER'S RAISIN-CRANBERRY PIE

Sandra Rodriguez, Provo, Utah

1 8-inch double crust pastry	1 cup granulated sugar
½ cup boiling water	3 tablespoons flour
¼ cup butter	1 teaspoon cinnamon
1 cup raisins, coarsely chopped	½ teaspoon nutmeg
1 cup cranberries, coarsely chopped	¼ teaspoon cloves
	1 teaspoon vanilla

Preheat oven to 350°F. Prepare pastry; line pie pan. In a medium bowl, combine boiling water and butter, stirring until butter is melted. Stir in raisins and cranberries; set aside. In a small bowl, combine sugar, flour, cinnamon, nutmeg, and cloves; mix well. Add dry mixture to raisin-cranberry mixture, mixing thoroughly. Stir in vanilla. Turn into pastry-lined pan. Cover top with crust, cutting slits for steam to escape. Seal and flute edge. Bake 50 minutes, covering edge with foil strip if it browns too much. Makes 8 servings.

CRANBERRY BREAD

Adele Williams, Athens, Georgia

2 cups sifted flour	1 tablespoon orange zest
½ teaspoon salt	5 tablespoons butter, divided
1½ teaspoons baking powder	1 egg, beaten
½ teaspoon baking soda	1 cup chopped walnuts
1 cup granulated sugar	1 cup chopped cranberries
¾ cup orange juice, plus 1 tablespoon	1½ cups confectioners' sugar
	1 tablespoon milk

Preheat oven to 350°F. Grease and flour a 9- x 5- x 3-inch loaf pan. In a large bowl, sift together flour, salt, baking powder, baking soda, and sugar; set aside. In a large measuring cup, combine ¾ cup orange juice, orange zest, and 2 tablespoons melted butter. Pour liquid into flour mixture; stir until dry ingredients are moistened. Add egg; stir until smooth. Fold in walnuts and cranberries. Turn batter into prepared pan. Bake 60 minutes or until toothpick inserted into the loaf comes out clean. Cool 5 minutes; turn out loaf on a wire rack. When cool, remove to a plate. In a small bowl, stir together confectioners' sugar, 3 tablespoons softened butter, 1 tablespoon orange juice, and milk. Drizzle glaze over loaf. Allow to set before slicing. Makes 8 servings.

SOMEONE TO REMEMBER

Patsy Evans Pittman

ROSE'S FAMILY

Over half a century has passed since I last saw Rose, but I will never forget her. She had soft gray curls, wore wire-rimmed glasses and would not think herself properly dressed unless she was wearing a Sunday dress, complete with lace collar and fair-sized pearls, or a print housedress with an apron, both with no-nonsense shoes. But what I most remember about Rose is that she was a doer of good deeds, quiet and unassuming.

Annie, Rose's youngest daughter, often baby-sat for me and my younger sister. I was almost four years old and my sister just a toddler when Rose volunteered to take us to Sunday school. I suspect that she considered it her duty to see that we "sweet babies" were adopted into her beloved church family. And so it came to pass that Rose, who had already raised five children, took on two more and yet another when my youngest sister was born.

Whatever the weather, on Sunday mornings Annie, with her mother beside her, drove up in the old blue Chevrolet to pick up the starched and polished little girls.

Those Sundays formed the framework of my life. I loved everything about Sunday school. I listened with rapt attention as the teacher told stories about David and Goliath and the little lost lamb and Mary and Joseph and Baby Jesus. As she talked, she slapped bright cutouts on a flannel board where they stuck as if by magic. But most of all, I loved the songs: "Climbing Jacob's Ladder," "This Little Light of Mine," and "Jesus Loves Me," my all-time favorite. I never doubted that the beautiful sanctuary, where light seemed to pour through the stained glass windows even on the gloomiest day, was indeed God's house.

On the way home, I would sing the songs, complete with all the motions, at the top of my voice. Rose just smiled.

By the time I was ten years old, I often walked the mile or so to Rose's house. She was always busy, but never in a hurry. I found that both com-

---

She was always busy, but never in a hurry.

---

forting and reassuring. I do not recall exactly what we ever talked about; but it seemed she was always there, in her apron, baking. And that was enough.

Recently, I found a recipe for Rose's sugar cookies in an old church cookbook; and it brought back all those memories of her warm, spicy kitchen and the huge cookies that seemed to have just been taken out of the oven whenever I arrived. Those cookies alone were enough to inspire a child's adoration. Like most good cooks, Rose assumed—wrongly I am afraid—that anyone would know just how much flour to add and how long and at what temperature to bake them.

I have been told that only two of Rose's grand-daughters have mastered the art.

In addition to cookies, Rose baked her own bread and hot rolls, which were as large as a small loaf of bread. They were both well worth the long walk to her house.

To supplement the family income, Rose took in laundry; and in the backyard, line after line of freshly washed clothes flapped in the wind. She often chuckled at the great number of half-dollars she received from her customers, since she had pledged all those particular coins to the Love Gift of her women's circle.

Rose also made quilts, and her quilting frame was a fixture in front of the dining room window. Since she charged only five dollars for each spool of thread used, her quilts surely must have been in great demand.

Pictures of her family, including a son and a daughter in uniform, lined the walls and broad windowsills of the house. With two of her children in service, I marvel now at Rose's serenity during the years of World War II. I only suppose that she had covered her children with her prayers and, unable to do more, surrendered them to God's care.

I was a junior in high school when Rose moved away. It was only a few miles but no longer within walking distance, and we gradually lost

Splatter ware pots and bowls of red apples add color to this farmhouse kitchen. Photograph by Jessie Walker.

touch. Perhaps that is how it was meant to be.

I like to believe she followed my progress as I grew up. One thing I do know: we could not have been as important to Rose as she was to us. This unpretentious woman had so much influence in nurturing the woman I became. Whether by chance or divine intervention, she came into our lives and blessed us with her faith and her quiet strength. "Thank you, Rose."

Since retiring, Patsy Evans Pittman's stories, poems, and essays have appeared in a variety of women's and inspirational publications, as well as several anthologies.

A Song of Gratitude

Grace Noll Crowell

Lord, You have been good to me,
Year long, life long;
I would sing the clearest, high
Glad thanksgiving song.

I would sing a song of praise
For the glory of the days,
For the years that I have spent:
Years of joy and deep content.
Lord, You have been good, so good;
My heart bursts with gratitude.

Lord, You have been good to me,
Caring for me ceaselessly.
Every prayer that I pray,
Every word that I say,
Everything that I do,
I would have them honor you.

Thanksgiving Inventory

Sudie Stuart Hager

I thank thee, Lord, for beauties such as these
Out of the dying year's abundant yield:
The first long strands on weeping willow trees,
The rich brown furrows of a newly plowed field,

Sunset clouds like chariots of fire,
A mountain lake of deep, mysterious blue,
Exultant music of a linnet choir,
The scent of roses, cool and fresh with dew,

Frost-turned maples in a hilltop row,
Bins of corn and dancing bonfire lights,
Arms of cedars, sagging under snow,
Drifts of wind-blown stars on clear, cold nights.

I thank thee, Lord, for beauties given me;
I pray I gave some lovely thing to Thee.

A country home in Linn County, Oregon, is bathed with soft evening light. Photograph by Steve Terrill.

49

HOMETOWN AMERICA

Dorothy Wallace

DIXON, CALIFORNIA

An island in a sea of beets" is the phrase once used by a local newspaperman to describe my hometown, located between San Francisco and Sacramento. The fertile land and the mild climate have always been important, but more important are the close ties to our neighbors. Only twenty-eight students were in my high school. When my friends and I were teenagers, we would meet on the banks of the Putah Creek to swim and picnic in the late spring. When we were not busy with chores, we invented many games to play together. Later, my two daughters both had the same kindergarten and third-grade teachers as I did, and thus I was kept well-informed about their progress.

The story of Dixon's origins illustrates the tradition of neighbors working together to create a better community. Thomas Dickson and his family came to this Central Valley region by covered wagon from Iowa, in 1853, with twelve head of oxen, three cows, and a few horses. Two other families soon arrived, and they named this little community Dicksonville.

Just a few miles away, a man named Elijah Silvey built an inn on the stagecoach route to Sacramento. By the mid-1860s, the town of Silveyville, which had grown up around the inn, had homes for 160 residents, a general store, a saloon, two churches, a school, and a blacksmith's shop.

In 1868, the California Pacific Railroad built tracks through land belonging to Dickson, who donated ten acres of his property for a station. Silveyville residents did not want to miss out on any economic opportunities and decided to move their entire community to Dicksonville. Proximity to the railroad would give the local farmers, and eventually dairymen and sheep ranchers, access to larger markets.

With the help of a newly arrived Danish cabinetmaker, people worked together to disassemble the town buildings. These were loaded onto large logs and pulled by forty-mule teams. As each building moved forward over the logs, groups of men shifted the last log out and moved it back underneath in front. The distance was only a few miles to the new tracks, but the relocation was not completed until 1871. Amazingly, the Methodist church, which still stands, continued to hold services every Sunday during its journey.

Early mail addressed to "Dixon," California, and a depot sign misspelled "Dixon" initiated the town's name change. Though some effort was made to correct the error, the new spelling remained.

May Day parades are always popular in Dixon, which has the oldest May Day Festival in the United States. Photograph courtesy of Dixon Public Library Archives.

Like those early settlers, my own family learned to adapt to change. My father returned from World War I with tuberculosis, and doctors informed him that he should never again work indoors. When he married Mother, a high school teacher, they moved from the downtown area to a small, two-bedroom home with fourteen acres, east of town. The house had what is called a "tank

---

People worked together to disassemble the town buildings.

---

house" on top to catch rain for water storage.

By 1923, our family had a large chicken house and we sold eggs. We all packed eggs in crates, and I will never forget the stiff feel of the burlap that we used to wrap them in order to keep them cool while they were being shipped. My younger brother and I were assigned chores, and my first responsibility was to shoo the chickens up to their roosts so that we could easily collect their eggs.

During the Depression, we always had enough eggs to make egg sandwiches to feed our family.

We learned how to raise sheep and grow crops such as beets, tomatoes, green peppers, corn, and alfalfa. We also built our own farm structures, including a mill for making mash for feed.

Many afternoons I walked the short distance from the school to the Dixon Carnegie Library to play with other children while we waited for our rides home. We entertained ourselves by taking turns sliding down the large banisters on the front steps. Built to be earthquake-safe, the library still stands today, and many generations of Dixon children have discovered those banisters too.

Remaining in a small hometown creates unique connections among the people. One daughter now lives in our original farmhouse and the other raised her family near here, in Davis. Even though the world has moved closer to Dixon, it has remained a small community with a determined spirit and strong family ties.

A Song of Thanks

Edward Smyth Jones

For the sun that shone at the dawn of spring,
For the flowers which bloom and the birds that sing,
For the verdant robe of the gray old earth,
For her coffers filled with their countless worth,
For the flocks which feed on a thousand hills,
For the rippling streams which turn the mills,
For the lowing herds in the lovely vale,
For the songs of gladness on the gale,
From the Gulf and the Lakes to the Oceans' banks,
Lord God of Hosts, we give Thee thanks!

For the farmer reaping his whitened fields,
For the bounty which the rich soil yields,
For the cooling dews and refreshing rains,
For the sun which ripens the golden grains,
For the bearded wheat and the fattened swine,
For the stalled ox and the fruitful vine,
For the tubers large and cotton white,
For the kid and the lambkin frisk and blithe,
For the swan which floats near the riverbanks,
Lord God of Hosts, we give Thee thanks!

For the lowly cot and the mansion fair,
For the peace and plenty together share,
For the Hand which guides us from above,
For Thy tender mercies, abiding love,
For the blessed home with its children gay,
For returnings of Thanksgiving Day,
For the bearing toils and the sharing cares,
We lift up our hearts in our songs and our prayers.
From the Gulf and the Lakes to the Oceans' banks,
Lord God of Hosts, we give Thee thanks!

*Birch and maple trees surround a house along Wyman Lake
in Somerset County, Maine. Photograph by Steve Terrill.*

FROM AMERICA'S ATTIC

D. Fran Morley and Maud Dawson

KEEPING IN TOUCH

"Watson, come here. I want you." With these words spoken to his assistant, Thomas Watson, in a rented room inside a machine shop in Boston, Massachusetts, Alexander Graham Bell launched a new invention on March 10, 1876, that changed communications in American society. Based on the design of the human ear, the new invention had been constructed by Bell and Watson from two disks connected by an electrified wire. By speaking into a funnel held close to the mouth, sound vibrations were transmitted through the wire to the other disk. "I now realize," Bell stated many years later, "that I should never have invented the telephone if I had been an electrician. What electrician would have been so foolish as to try any such thing? The advantage I had was that sound had been the study of my life—the study of vibrations."

Bell, who would be awarded the patent for his invention on his twenty-ninth birthday, was born and educated in Scotland. After the death of two of his brothers from tuberculosis, Bell and his parents moved to Canada. A third-generation specialist in human speech, Bell was fascinated by efforts to help mute people learn speech. The Boston Board of Education, having learned of Bell's reputation, offered him five hundred dollars to move to Boston and introduce his methods at a school for deaf-mutes. Bell became a professor at Boston University and soon opened a school of his own. One of his pupils was a young girl named Mabel Hubbard whose father would later provide the business acumen and financial backing to help Bell, as well as allow Mabel to become Bell's wife.

Bell made the first long-distance telephone call to his father and uncle.

Bell, who had been working on a telegraph that would send and receive multiple messages, began to focus on the mechanics of sound reproduction and made a profound discovery: "If I can get a mechanism which will make a current of electricity vary in its intensity as the air varies in density when a sound is passing through it, I can telegraph any sound, even the sound of speech." Based on this theory, he and Watson created the telephone.

Hubbard made arrangements for Bell to display his new invention at the Philadelphia Centennial Exposition of 1876. For several weeks, the invention did not attract anyone's notice. Then the Emperor of Brazil, who had visited Bell's classroom at Boston University and also had founded a school for deaf-mutes in Rio De Janeiro, recognized Bell and insisted upon a demonstration of the telephone. Bell recited through the telephone Hamlet's "To be or not to be" soliloquy and impressed a nearby group of exhibition judges. Bell was given a Certificate of Award for achieving "a result of transcendent scientific interest."

Afterward, the momentum of the new invention was enormous. Bell made the first long-distance telephone call to his father and uncle in Ontario on borrowed telegraph lines; and the first two-way long distance conversation over an outdoor wire was made between Bell and Watson from Cambridge to Boston. But 1877 brought even more changes. Bell, his father-in-law, and other financial backers formed Bell Telephone. Hubbard, after having first offered to sell the telephone to Western Union Telegraph Company for $100,000, decided to lease the equipment and license franchises instead. And the first telephone system, called an exchange, was opened in New Haven, Connecticut. In a few years, other exchanges were opened in every major city in the United States.

The first exchange operators answered incoming calls at a large switchboard and connected the customers manually. The first operators were teenage boys, who had been good employees for telegraph companies. But in 1878, in Boston, an exchange began hiring women, who were thought to have more pleasant voices and who were paid about seven dollars a week.

One problem that soon arose with the acceptance of the telephone was the form of greeting that should be used when a person answered a call. Bell favored and continued to use his expression "Hoy! Hoy!" Others tried, and dismissed, "What is wanted?" and "Are you ready to talk?" Thomas Edison then came up with "Hello," which the telephone businessmen considered "undignified" but the public immediately adopted. By 1880, at

A cradle phone was an important addition to a household of the 1930s. Photograph by H. Armstrong Roberts/H. Armstrong Roberts.

the first National Convention of Telephone Companies, attendees wore badges with "Hello" printed on them. Mark Twain's comic sketch, "A Telephone Conversation," written in the same year, also used the word and helped to establish it. Soon AT&T, a subsidiary of Bell Telephone, began to promote its switchboard operators as "hello girls."

From a crank wall phone to cradle desk phones or the popular pastel princess phones, the design has evolved as improvements in technology were implemented. Today's palm-sized devices provide strains of classical or pop music and can be tucked into our purses or attached to belts. We can send and receive text messages and pictures via telephone keypads, and we can schedule our lives by using a telephone's calendar or clock. We no longer need to be isolated from our family or lonely for the voice of a friend. A simple "hello" is just the beginning of keeping in touch with those important to our lives.

Father, We Thank Thee

Rebecca J. Weston

Father, we thank Thee for the night,
And for the pleasant morning light,
For rest and food and loving care,
And all that makes the world so fair.

Help us to do the things we should,
To be to others kind and good,
In all we do in work and play
To love Thee better day by day.

Thanksgiving

John Oxenham

For all things beautiful and good and true;
For things that seemed not good yet turned to good;
For all the sweet compulsions of Thy will
That chastened, tried, and wrought us to Thy shape;
For things unnumbered that we take of right
And value first when they are withheld;
For light and air; sweet sense of sound and smell;
For ears to hear the heavenly harmonies;
For eyes to see the unseen in the seen;
For vision of the Worker in the work;
For hearts to apprehend Thee everywhere—
We thank Thee, Lord.

Love's Prayer

James Whitcomb Riley

Dear Lord! Kind Lord!
    Gracious Lord! I pray
Thou wilt look on all I love,
    Tenderly today!
Weed their hearts of weariness;
    Scatter every care
Down a wake of angel wings
    Winnowing the air.

Bring unto the sorrowing
    All release from pain;
Let the lips of laughter
    Overflow again;
And with all the needy
    O divide, I pray,
This vast treasure of content
    That is mine today!

The stone edifice of The United Methodist Church of Springfield, Vermont, has imposing twin steeples. Photograph by William H. Johnson.

THROUGH MY WINDOW

Pamela Kennedy

THE FABRIC OF FAMILY

When the Thanksgiving table is set and we all gather around to share our favorite dishes, we inevitably begin to share our favorite memories too. The cranberry relish is Great-Grandma's recipe; and someone always brings up the year the cranberries inexplicably exploded, plastering the oven interior with sticky red bomblets. Then there was the holiday when Great-Grandpa entertained the youngsters by removing his dentures and whistling the "Star-Spangled Banner"! This story is usually followed with the one recalling how Aunt Katie's horseradish-spiked tomato aspic precipitated familial coughing spasms and a collective mad dash for the ice water. The fabric of our family wraps around us as we share anecdotes that link current generations with those long gone. It feels good to have this ongoing conversation, to laugh together and enjoy our heritage, to be warmed by this blanket of love.

This year, there will be new stories to add as we give thanks for the life of my mother-in-law, Arlene, who left our family circle last March. But this time we will share more than just the family reminiscences, for we have received a great outpouring of memories from her community to weave together with our own. In the months since last spring, we have discovered so many new things to be thankful for about this dear lady we all loved so much.

A young mother shared how she used to go to the neighborhood market after her children were all asleep and her husband was home to watch them. On several occasions she encountered Arlene, a dedicated night owl, near the produce section. Between the broccoli and the Brussels sprouts, the two women talked about

She composed at least two or three handwritten notes almost every day of her life.

life. My mother-in-law was never too tired or too rushed to offer encouragement, to share a hug or a tear with the younger woman, who said that those late-night "counseling sessions" gave her hope and enabled her to handle daily challenges.

A successful businessman related that the foundation for his commitment to God was laid in the basement of Arlene's house on Tuesday afternoons where she held a weekly "Know Your Bible Club" for thirty years. Boys and girls were challenged to memorize Scripture, while flannelgraph presentations of Bible stories helped them explore valuable life lessons. Now nearing forty, this businessman could still recite those Scripture passages he had memorized, and he shares the Bible stories he learned at their age with his own children.

Dianne, who came now and then to clean Arlene's house, told us how when she was dusting or shining a mirror, she often heard my mother-in-law's voice from another room. But when Dianne went to see what Arlene wanted, she found the older woman alone, earnestly conversing with God about one of her friends in need.

Arlene was always having a conversation with someone. She never met a stranger. At times, much to the family's dismay, she would follow an initial greeting with very personal questions, such as "Why, I have never seen you serving at this restaurant before. How attractive you are. Is there a special young man in your life?" or "You are awfully young to be a surgeon. Do you mind telling me a bit about your family and background? Do you go to church anywhere special?" Although my husband was often chagrined by his mother's outgoing and inquisitive personality, her genuine interest and concern about people caused them to open up to her like flowers in the sun. She had friends everywhere, and she corresponded with most of them. E-mails and instant messages were not for her. Instead, she composed at least two or three handwritten notes almost every day of her life.

We used to tease her when she insisted that we take her mail directly to the main Post Office, which was five miles away, when there was a perfectly good mailbox right across the street.

"You never know when the mailman will come and pick up that mail over there," she would respond, pointing disdainfully in the direction of the big blue box. "My letters will go out at least a day faster from the main terminal." When we argued that her little notes were probably not time critical, she looked at us with disapproval. "You do not know how long it feels when you are waiting for a word of encouragement."

And she was right. At her memorial service, several people came up to members of the family clutching notes they had received weeks, years, even decades, earlier. They all wanted to read a sentence or two and to share how her words had reached them "at just the right time" to lift spirits, bring hope, or heal a hurt.

This Thanksgiving, we will gather again at the table and weave more stories into the fabric of our family. Although our circle will be a bit smaller, our hearts will be fuller, for there is no greater reason to give thanks than for a life well lived.

Pamela Kennedy is a freelance writer of short stories, articles, essays, and children's books. Wife of a retired naval officer and mother of three children, she has made her home on both U.S. coasts and currently resides in Honolulu, Hawaii.

Original artwork by Doris Ettlinger.

After Thanksgiving
Amy Dengler

Family remain at the table,
    quiet in their chairs,
    passing memories left to right,
    everyone reaching for what he loves most.
The damask cloth, twice handed down,
    sustains saturations of gravy and tea,
    little stuck buttons of wax.
After dinner, we women stir ourselves
    into a lively epilogue—scraping, sorting,
    shivering the last of the cranberries
    from the cut-glass bowl,
    consigning the feast to foil.
Already sunset has gone without our noticing,
    darkness making a mirror
    of the window over the sink.
We peer through to the reflected cityscape
    stacking up on the kitchen table:
    candlesticks like church spires,
    the good china and crystal towering over crumpled
    pyramids of white linen.
In the sequence of sudsing up glass and silver,
    conversations condense on the window,
    bubbles rise to opalesce the air
    over the clear rinse of completion.

WE CAN ONLY BE SAID TO BE ALIVE
IN THOSE MOMENTS WHEN OUR HEARTS
ARE CONSCIOUS OF OUR TREASURES.
—THORNTON WILDER

This Federal style Colonial dining room features a cherry dining table and mustard-colored paneling. Photograph by Jessie Walker.

The Twilight of Thanksgiving

William D. Kelley

The day has lengthened into eve,
And over all the meadows
The twilight's silent shuttles weave
Their somber web of shadows;
With northern lights the cloudless skies
Are faintly phosphorescent,
And just above yon wooded rise
The new moon shows her crescent.

Before the evening lamps are lit,
While day and night commingle,
The sire and matron come and sit
Beside the cozy ingle
And softly speak of the delight
Within their bosoms swelling
Because beneath their roof tonight
Their dear ones all are dwelling.

And when around the cheerful blaze
The young folks take their places,
What blissful dreams of other days
Light up their aged faces!

The past returns with all its joys,
And they again are living
The years in which, as girls and boys,
Their children kept Thanksgiving.

The stalwart son recalls the time
When, urged to the endeavor,
He tried the well-greased pole to climb
And failed of fame forever.
The daughter tells of her emprise
When, as a new beginner,
She helped her mother make the pies
For the Thanksgiving dinner.

And thus with laugh and jest and song
And tender recollections,
Love speeds the happy hours along
And fosters fond affections;
While Fancy, listening to the mirth,
And dreaming pleasant fictions,
Imagines through the winds on earth
That heaven breathes benedictions.

*The muted hues of dried flowers soften the ceiling
of this family room. Photograph by Jessie Walker.*

DEVOTIONS FROM THE HEART

Pamela Kennedy

Do not be anxious about anything, but in everything, by prayer and petition, with thanksgiving, present your requests to God. And the peace of God, which transcends all understanding, will guard your hearts and your minds in Christ Jesus. —Philippians 4:6-7 (NIV)

NEED PEACE—GIVE THANKS!

I just do not know what we are going to do if Jim loses his job," my friend lamented.

"I am not sure we can afford to send Jenny to college. Our savings were eaten up when I had emergency surgery last spring," another confided.

"Mother and Dad are not doing well, and they refuse to accept any help or even to consider moving to a retirement apartment," a couple in our prayer group shared.

Sometimes, life may seem as if it were filled with worries. Anxiety-producing situations abound, and simple solutions elude us. Even if our lives seem to be moving along smoothly, when we pick up a newspaper or turn on the television we are confronted with news that may overwhelm us with hopelessness and despair. What can we do? Where can we turn? Is there really a silver lining behind all the dark clouds crowding the horizon?

Our hearts long for peace, but it may seem a futile dream. Or is it? The Apostle Paul, although he lived almost two thousand years ago, faced concerns much like ours. He battled worries about health and hardships, about relationships and natural disasters. But he also discovered and shared with us the antidote for a fretful life.

In the verses above, Paul commands his Philippian friends to turn their backs on anxiety by turning their faces toward God in prayer. But the type of prayer he prescribes is not composed of vague or repetitious phrases uttered in the hopes of a brighter day. Paul urges followers to pray aggressively, specifically, and confidently to a living God. Paul's advice is a cure linked to a prom-

---

Dear Lord, I confess that I often look at my worries instead of Your abundant love. Help me remember that You promise peace when I bring You my prayers with thanksgiving.

---

ise—a promise that gives us the means to break the debilitating cycle of worry. First, Paul tells us to present our requests to God through prayers and petitions. This indicates an active and specific recounting of our desires and needs. But then Paul indicates how these requests are to be made: with thanksgiving. Have you ever thought about giving thanks for what you do not have? For instance, if you had a debt to pay off, but you also had a large balance in the bank, would you not be thankful as you wrote out the check? As we bring our requests to God, Paul wants us to remember that our heavenly Father has all the resources in the universe at His disposal and He has given us, His children, a blank check. When we choose to stop worrying and to write out the check by prayerfully presenting our needs, we express the confidence that the resources needed are available to us. It is then that the thankfulness of grateful children floods our souls. We have a Father who loves us and desires to fill our lives with what He knows will fulfill us. What could produce more gratitude than that?

Gratitude permits us to experience the truth of the second part of Paul's statement: God's peace—a peace so great that we cannot even comprehend it—will guard our hearts and minds in Christ Jesus. When we present our needs, thankful that our Lord is fully able to meet every one, our worries are overcome by the assurance of God's peace.

Red-hued maple leaves and one perfect apple decorate this charming window seat. Photograph by Jessie Walker.

At Thanksgiving, it is good to remember that we cannot only be thankful for the tangible blessings of family and friends gathered around a bountiful table, but that we can also enjoy the invisible and eternal blessings of God's abundant love and provision through prayer. If you are in need of peace this holiday season, try giving thanks. Then prepare yourself to receive blessings beyond your understanding!

Red Chimneys

Grace Noll Crowell

A chimney is to any house
What fire is to a hearth
Or what the warm gold sun is
To the old gray earth.

I have seen a chimney tip
A roof with scarlet light,
As if one set lit candles on
A sill at night.

I have seen them gleam and glow
Against the morning sky,
Like red birds waiting in the mist
Before they fly.

I have watched blue spiraled smoke
Lift up a windblown flower
From bright red chimneys to denote
Men's supper hour.

Chimneys are to any house
What lamps are to the night;
Unto each heart, some chimney is
A beacon light.

The Woodpile

Creta Smith

A woodpile possesses beauty
That is unique, its own.
I admire its grace and color,
Its texture, depth, and tone.
Within its heart are warmth
    and strength,
Constancy and comfort rare;
One of nature's purest products,
It's stacked with farmers' care.
I feel there's nothing lovelier
Than the yard draped with snow
And to see from our own window
The wood piled row on row.

A sugar maple tree protects a woodpile near Sutton, New Hampshire. Photograph by William H. Johnson.

The Fireplace
Hal Borland

Philosophy and faith are companions at the hearth, and ever have been.

There are better ways to heat a house, but neither love nor friendship is too much concerned with economics. Man built a home around a fire, and there the family grew. To his fireside man brought his friends, and friendship grew, and understanding. So hearth became home, and home became heart. It has little changed over the centuries. What greater friendship or understanding is there than that which stands, back to hearth, and faces outer cold and darkness unafraid?

A roaring fire warms this cozy living room.
Photograph by Jessie Walker.

READERS' REFLECTIONS

Readers are invited to submit original poetry for possible publication in future issues of IDEALS. Please send typed copies only; manuscripts will not be returned. Writers receive payment for each published submission. Send material to Readers' Reflections, Ideals Publications, 535 Metroplex Drive, Suite 250, Nashville, Tennessee 37211.

Whisperings

Meagan Nagy
Fairfield, California

As a stillness settles upon the air,
With a flick of winter's wand,
A hard shell forms over the land
Sealing in the warmth of summer.
So I go inward to a cozier place,
Nestled beside a crackling fire.
The blaze reflects and flickers in my eyes;
And I become lost in its glow,
Hypnotized by the dancing flames.
In the vast, stark wilderness of my mind
Skaters dance and float over the ice
Beneath a sky filled with holes

Through which a million tiny lights shine.
Drifting effortlessly into the night,
I no longer hear the sounds of burning logs,
Their snapping, sizzling lullaby
That led me to this place.
Nor am I aware
Of the downy soft pillow forming on the sill,
Too cool for me to lay my dreamy head.
Tomorrow will be filled
With a clean, white newness;
Its canvas awaits me.

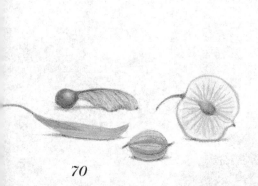

Bittersweet Walk
Phyllis Evola
Murfreesboro, Tennessee

I walked in the woods on a chill autumn morn;
The leaves crunched beneath my feet, ragged and torn.
The dampness wrapped around my shoulders like a cloak;
My feet felt the cold as the shoe leather became soaked.
A gray mist hung in the air, shrouding the sun;
At last, in the distance, I spotted my find and began to run.
Bittersweet is what prompted my walk among the trees;
There it was, as if to say, "Take me, please."
When I arrive home, to my chair I retire
And admire my bouquet in front of the fire.
I savor the pleasure I cannot hide,
Mesmerized by the red autumn flames here inside.

Announcement
Raymond D. Humphrey
Grand Blanc, Michigan

The maple, oak, and hickory
Stand barren of their leaves;
Golden grain cut down in prime
Is gathered in its sheaves;
The shocks of corn are bundled,
Rows of one by one;
The scarecrow's job is done;
Melancholy gives way to cheer
As nature rearranges the seasons of the year.
Thanksgiving Day is here!

Fireside
Debra Schademann
West Point, Nebraska

A cozy place to be,
Sitting by the fire,
I watch the flames
Leap to and fro;
Sparks jump as if
They want to
Touch the sky.
The smell of burning logs
Brings me back
To those times of
Marshmallows and hot dogs,
Friends and family.
Oh, how I love to sit
By the fire and
Reminisce of those
Times of long ago.

Old Song
Edward Fitzgerald

'Tis a dull sight
    To see the year dying,
When winter winds
    Set the yellow wood sighing:
      Sighing, O sighing!

When such a time cometh,
    I do retire
Into an old room
    Beside a bright fire:
      O, pile a bright fire!

And there I sit
    Reading old things,
Of knights and lorn damsels,
    While the wind sings—
      O, drearily sings!

I never look out
    Nor attend to the blast;
For all to be seen
    Is the leaves falling fast:
      Falling, falling!

But close at the hearth,
    Like a cricket, sit I,
Reading of summer
    And chivalry—
      Gallant chivalry!

A Book
Emily Dickinson

There is no frigate like a book
To take us away,
Nor any coursers like a page
Of prancing poetry.
This traverse may the poorest take
Without oppress of toll;
How frugal is the chariot
That bears a human soul!

Words
Charles Harpur

Words are deeds. The words we hear
May revolutionize or rear
A mighty state. The words we read
May be a spiritual deed
Excelling any fleshly one,
As much as the celestial sun
Transcends a bonfire made to throw
A light upon some raree show.
A simple proverb tagged with rhyme
May color half the course of time;
The pregnant saying of a sage
May influence every coming age;
A song in its effects may be
More glorious than Thermopylae,
And many a lay that schoolboys scan
A nobler feat than Inkerman.

*A young lady relaxes with a favorite book in this painting entitled
A QUIET READ by Alfred Augustus Glendening. Image from Fine Art
Photographic Library, Ltd., London/N. Drummond.*

BITS & PIECES

To sit alone in the lamplight with a book spread out before you
and hold intimate converse with men of unseen generations—
such is a pleasure beyond compare.
> —*Yoshida Kenko*

Give a man a book he can read:
And his home is bright with a calm delight,
Though the room be poor indeed.
> —*James Thomson*

At night, when the curtains are
drawn and the fire flickers, my books
attain a collective dignity.
> —*E. M. Forster*

How am I to sing your praise,
Happy chimney-corner days,
Sitting safe in nursery nooks,
Reading picture storybooks?
> —*Robert Louis Stevenson*

*I*t is not true that we have only one life to live: if we can read, we can live as many more lives and as many kinds of lives as we wish.

—*S. I. Hayakawa*

*E*very man who knows how to read has it in his power to magnify himself, to multiply the ways in which he exists, to make his life full, significant, interesting.

—*Aldous Huxley*

*J*ust the knowledge that a good book is awaiting one at the end of a long day makes that day happier.

—*Kathleen Norris*

*I*t is a man's duty to have books. A library is not a luxury, but one of the necessities of life.

—*Henry Ward Beecher*

*W*hen you read a classic you do not see in the book more than you did before. You see more in you than was there before.

—*Clifton Fadiman*

Dust of Snow
Robert Frost

The way a crow　　　Has given my heart
Shook down on me　　A change of mood
The dust of snow　　And saved some part
From a hemlock tree　Of a day I had rued.

The Promise
Elaine Porter

Walking at dusk, the first snow
Fluffy beneath my booted feet,
I see a giant oak ahead,
Bare arms outstretched, as if
Imploring winter to be merciful.
As I draw closer my hearing sharpens,
And I become aware of light wind
Rustling through the few dried leaves
That cling here and there.

I sense a whispering on the breeze,
Assuring that towering, venerable tree:
"Hold on, dear friend, hold on.
The beauty of snowflakes yet to come
Will sustain your spirit,
And enough sun will keep hopes high
Until warmth and new growth draw nigh."

And in that frosty stillness,
I feel those gentle words whisper
As much to me as to that tree.

Ring of Seasons
Mary Catherine Johnson

After autumn's early snow
Has fallen whither will it go,
　　The woods are full of sound:
An evening owl's inquiring hoot,
The squeak of snow beneath a boot,
　　A rabbit's muted bound.

Laden branches crack and fall;
The wind conveys the coyote's call
　　Down from the mountain's brink.
A portion of the creek is clear
Of ice, and there the trembling deer
　　Come cautiously to drink.

The winter forest resonates
With life and patiently awaits
　　The rolling of the ring
When ice will thaw and snow will melt,
And summer can be faintly felt
　　Trailing after spring.

Melting snow lies on bright fall leaves on this forest floor near Franconia, New Hampshire. Photograph by William H. Johnson.

LET WINTER COME

Sudie Stuart Hager

Let winter come. The year has brought
    A springtime rare and long,
A rainbow-tinted world brimful
    Of laughter, blooms, and song;
A June of radiant loveliness,
    A wedding in her train,
Fruit that ripened rich and full
    In summer sun and rain;
Golden autumn days with clouds
    Too thin to mar the blue;
Oh, He who made these seasons bright
    Will bless the winter too.

FIRST SNOW

Bessie Saunders Spencer

The dusk has hidden the golden stars
And north wind leaps through the pasture bars.
A small boy fastens an outer shed
And stops to polish a bright blue sled.
A dog is slipped through the kitchen door,
With quick repairs to the tidy floor.
A cap and a muffler are on the chair,
And strange expectancy is in the air.
He walks and watches and softly hums
And sings aloud as the first snow comes.

*An early snow has blanketed this wood in Oconto County, Wisconsin.
Photograph by Darryl E. Beers.*

SLICE OF LIFE

Edna Jaques

COUNTRY LIVING

I think that country living finds its peak
In wintertime when fields are wrapped in snow,
When cellars bulge with little stored up things,
Barrels of salt pork, fruit standing row on row,
Bins of potatoes, apples in their prime;
For gracious living, give me wintertime.

The summer's rush is over on the land:
Crops gathered in, sleek cattle in their stalls,
The sheep well housed, chickens contented like,
While over all a sense of quiet falls
As if the earth were taking a short nap
Like an old woman in a woolen wrap.

The hills are white against the winter sky,
The meadows bedded down for winter sleep,
Old maple trees rock stiffly in the wind,
Around the farmhouse purple shadows creep,
A lighted window sends a shaft of light
Into the darkness of the winter night.

How good a life can be that holds unto
The sane and simple ways of Mother Earth,
Whose days are lived with piety and grace,
Acquainted with the ways of death and birth,
Yet holding ever in its calloused hand
The quiet strength and beauty of the land.

These cabins stand at the edge of the forest in Government Camp in Mount Hood National Forest, Oregon. Photograph by Steve Terrill.

AMID THE STORM

Melody Lee-Carte

As winter comes upon the land,
The cool breeze begins to blow.
I snuggle by the fireplace;
Outside it starts to snow.
I am warm inside my cabin,
Hidden deep in the woods.
The ground is a blanket of white
Where beautiful flowers once stood.
The clouds begin to rumble;
The winds are thrashing around;

The snow is swiftly flying,
Yet there is hardly a sound.
I look outside my window:
A scene of frozen landscape,
With icicles sparkling, bold;
The snow envelops my soul.
I witness a wonderful mystery
Where Mother Nature is reborn.
I reach to pet my kitten,
Knowing we are safe and warm.

COUNTRY CABIN

Dell Dean

North winds are howling as winter draws near.
Wild geese flock southward till spring of next year.
The leaves have all fallen; our fruit trees look dead.
Old Mister Bear's dug himself a snug bed.
Out in the smokehouse hang bacon and hams;
My wife's been busy with canning and jams.
Plenty of firewood's been stacked by the door;
Inside a warm rug covers our floor.
Dusk is approaching and supper's being made;
We share fried pork chops while fresh biscuits bake.

Later this evening we'll build up the fire,
Snug as that bear in his warm forest lair.
Lulled by the winds in their rhythmic chanting,
We eagerly plan next year's planting.
Hard rains are due soon, then snow
    through the night;
Morning should bring us a world covered white.
But stout is our cabin, as strong as our love,
As we kneel to give thanks to our Lord above.

Eternal Journey
Chris Roe

As the crimson flame of life
Breaks slowly
Above the horizon,
The white, frosted meadows
With trees and hedgerows
Of sculptured ice
Speak loudly of Your presence.

Once more upon this journey,
Without effort or intrusion,
Through the peace and tranquility
Of Your silent voice,
The moment becomes eternal
And the journey
Begins again.

Until the Spring
Ethel Green Russell

The scarlet leaves
Are falling fast;
The autumn now
Is almost past,

And as each red
Leaf disappears
Beneath
The snowflakes' icy tears,

The winter's cold
Once more will bring
White radiance
To everything.

Here will I wait
Until the spring
Renews each hope
With blossoming.

*Fresh snow highlights tall fir trees on the Molas Divide of the San Juan Range
in San Juan National Forest, Colorado. Photograph by Jeff Gnass.*

READERS' FORUM

Snapshots from our IDEALS readers

Top left: Gracey and Kelby York, daughters of James and Heather York and granddaughters of Mike and Denise Wright, all of Jamestown, Tennessee, are taking a drive in their Volkswagen convertible. Cousin Maggie Wright also enjoys the ride.

Below left: Six-year-old Lucas Ridall, son of Gary and Linda Ridall of Carlisle, Pennsylvania, loves to play in the leaves at his grandmother Marion Ridall's yard in Orangeville.

Below: "Another flash?" Arlene and Willie Grewe of Arlington Heights, Illinois, share this picture of their great-grandson, David Peter Grewe, who has already learned to pose for a photographer.

Right: "Howdy, partner," says two-year-old Jack Ireland as he enjoys an afternoon at the county fair. Jack is the son of Jarrod and Christa Ireland of Garden Grove, California.

Below: "Pumpkins and more pumpkins! Oh, my!" says fifteen-month-old Trevor White. His great-great-aunt, Eileen Huber of Morton, Illinois, shares this picture with IDEALS readers.

THANK YOU for sharing your family photographs with IDEALS. We hope to hear from other readers who would like to share snapshots with the IDEALS family. Please include a self-addressed, stamped envelope if you would like the photos returned; or keep your original photographs for safekeeping and send duplicate photos along with your name, address, and telephone number to:

Readers' Forum
Ideals Publications
535 Metroplex Drive, Suite 250
Nashville, Tennessee 37211

Dear Reader,

When I was young, Thanksgiving was a day of family. I remember preparing dinner in the kitchen with my mother, grandmother, aunt, and sometimes a neighbor or friend. There I first felt the warm friendship of women creating food for their loved ones.

During those years, I learned how to make turkey stuffing. Several weeks before Thanksgiving, Mother froze leftover homemade cornbread and biscuits. My job was to crumble these into a large bowl. I also chopped onions and celery and put them in a pot to boil. My grandmother added broth; only she could judge the proper amount. The appropriate measure of sage remains a mystery to me. No matter how careful I am, I somehow put a little too much, or not quite enough, sage in my dressing.

This ritual shared with my grandmother and mother is important and remains with me. Now my daughter and I stand shoulder to shoulder in the kitchen at Thanksgiving crumbling homemade cornbread, stirring in the broth, and searching for just the right amount of sage for the perfect Thanksgiving dinner.

Marjorie L. Lloyd

Publisher, Patricia A. Pingry
Editor, Marjorie Lloyd
Sr. Designer, Marisa Calvin
Copy Editor, Marie Brown
Permissions Editor, Patsy Jay
Contributing Writers, Maud Dawson, Joan Donaldson, Pamela Kennedy, D. Fran Morley, Patsy Evans Pittman, and Dorothy Wallace

ACKNOWLEDGMENTS

BORLAND, HAL. An excerpt from *This Hill, This Valley,* Copyright © 1957 by Hal Borland. Used by permission of Frances Collin, Literary Agent. BUTLER, EDITH SHAW. "Definition." Used by permission of Nancy B. Truesdell. CROWELL, GRACE NOLL. "Red Chimneys" and "A Song of Gratitude" from *Silver In the Sun.* Copyright © 1927 and renewed 1955 by Grace Noll Crowell. Used by permission of HarperCollins Publishers. DICKINSON, EMILY. "Autumn" from *The Poems of Emily Dickinson,* edited by Ralph W. Franklin, Cambridge, Mass.: The Belknap Press of Harvard University Press, Copyright © 1951, 1955, 1979, 1983 1998 by the President and Fellows of Harvard College. Reprinted by permission of the publishers and the Trustees of Amherst College. FASSLER, EDITH. "A Song of Autumn." Used by permission of John Fassler. FROST, FRANCES M. "Apple Song" from *Pool In the Meadow.* Copyright © 1933 by the author, renewed © 1961 by Sister Marguerite. Reprinted by permission of Houghton Mifflin Company. FROST, ROBERT. "Dust Of Snow" from *The Poetry of Robert Frost,* edited by Edward Connery Lathem. Copyright © 1951 by the author. Copyright © 1923 and 1969 by Henry Holt and Co. Reprinted by permission of the publisher. GWYNNE, J. HAROLD. "Twilight." Used by permission of Ruth Gwynne Dullien. HOWARD, STARRLETTE. "Thanksgiving On the Farm." Used by permission of Maxine H. Smith. JARRELL, MILDRED L. "Indian Summer." Used by permission of Serena Naumann. OXENHAM, JOHN. "Thanksgiving." Used by permission of Desmond Dunkerley. SPENCER, BESSIE SAUNDERS. "First Snow." Originally appeared in *Good Housekeeping.* Submitted by the author. STRONG, PATIENCE. "Coming Home." Used by permission of Rupert Crew Ltd.
We sincerely thank those authors, or their heirs, some of whom we were unable to locate, who submitted original poems or articles to *Ideals* for publication. Every possible effort has been made to acknowledge ownership of material used.

This watercolor entitled STILL LIFE WITH GRAPES IN A VASE *by Pierre-Joseph Redouté (1759–1840) softens the colors of autumn fruit. Image from Art Resource, NY/Réunion des Musées Nationaux.*

The Blessings of
CHRISTMAS

ideals

"Christmas is the day that holds all time together."
—Alexander Smith

The beautiful and inspiring pages of *THE BLESSINGS OF CHRISTMAS* will help you recall the warm moments and countless blessings of the season. Rejoice in the tender poems, inspirational stories, classic hymns, and heartfelt prayers that are featured throughout this magnificent book.

Over eighty brilliant color photographs and paintings inspire new meaning for this special time of year. Eight chapters celebrate the many blessings of the season, from time shared with our families to the birth of Christ.

CHAPTER HIGHLIGHTS —

° *Blessings of Home*—Henry Van Dyke's beautiful *"A Christmas Prayer for the Home"*

° *Blessings of Family*—Louisa May Alcott's warm story *"Learning the Truth of the Christmas Spirit"*

° *Blessings of Friends*—Marjorie Holmes recounts the joy *"In Praise of Christmas Letters"*

° *Blessings of Angels*—Rejoice in the beloved carol, *"Angels We Have Heard on High"*

° *Blessings of Shepherds*—Samuel Taylor Coleridge's tender poem *"The Shepherds"*

° *Blessings of Magi*—Lola S. Morgan's touching poem *"The Wise Men's Story"*

° *Blessings of Jesus*—Henry Vaughan's exhortation *"Christ's Nativity"*

° *Blessings of Peace*—Henry Wadsworth Longfellow's joyous poem *"Christmas Bells"*

Simply complete and return the reply card today to preview *THE BLESSINGS OF CHRISTMAS* for 21 days FREE.... and receive a FREE *Christmas Poems* booklet.

Christmas Poems

FREE GIFT

Yours just for ordering!

Guideposts

DAILY PLANNER
2006

What will you remember in the coming year?

Celebrate God's presence in your life as you keep track of important daily appointments, birthdays, anniversaries, holidays and more with the *Guideposts Daily Planner, 2006*.

This beautifully-designed hardcover book not only provides plenty of space to track the important details of your days, it also gives you the means to jot down your prayer requests, note when your prayers have been answered and track the living proof of divine influence in your life.

Filled with soul-stirring stories, life-affirming Bible verses, and prayers for deepening and enriching your faith...there simply has never been a better way to keep track of personal and spiritual commitments all in one perfect place!

In the weeks and months that lie ahead, so much is going to happen. Begin 2006 with a simple journey of self-discovery that will show you how God works in your life...each and every day!

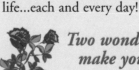 *Two wonderful ways to make your days a delight!*

Guideposts created an exclusive *Daily Planner 2006* and the **FREE** *Pocket Planner*—the very first date book designed to manage your prayer life along with your personal life!

Complete the Free Examination Certificate and mail today for your 30-Day Preview. And receive a FREE GUIDEPOSTS POCKET PLANNER 2006 just for ordering.

This wonderful FREE gift is the perfect way to take your schedule of appointments and inspirational verses with you.

FREE EXAMINATION CERTIFICATE

YES! I'd like to examine *Guideposts Daily Planner, 2006*, at no risk or obligation. If I decide to keep the book, I will be billed later at the low Guideposts price of only $12.95, plus shipping and processing. If not completely satisfied, I may return the book within 30 days and owe nothing. The FREE *Pocket Planner* is mine to keep no matter what I decide.

Total copies ordered: _____

Please print your name and address:

_____
NAME

_____
ADDRESS   APT#

_____
CITY   STATE   ZIP

Allow 4 weeks for delivery. Orders subject to credit approval.
Send no money now. We will bill you later.
www.Guideposts.org

Printed in USA
14/202366454

Guideposts
POCKET PLANNER
2006

YOURS
FREE

Send for a risk-free home trial today!